FORMS OF GOVERNMENT: NEED TO KNOW

COMMUNISM

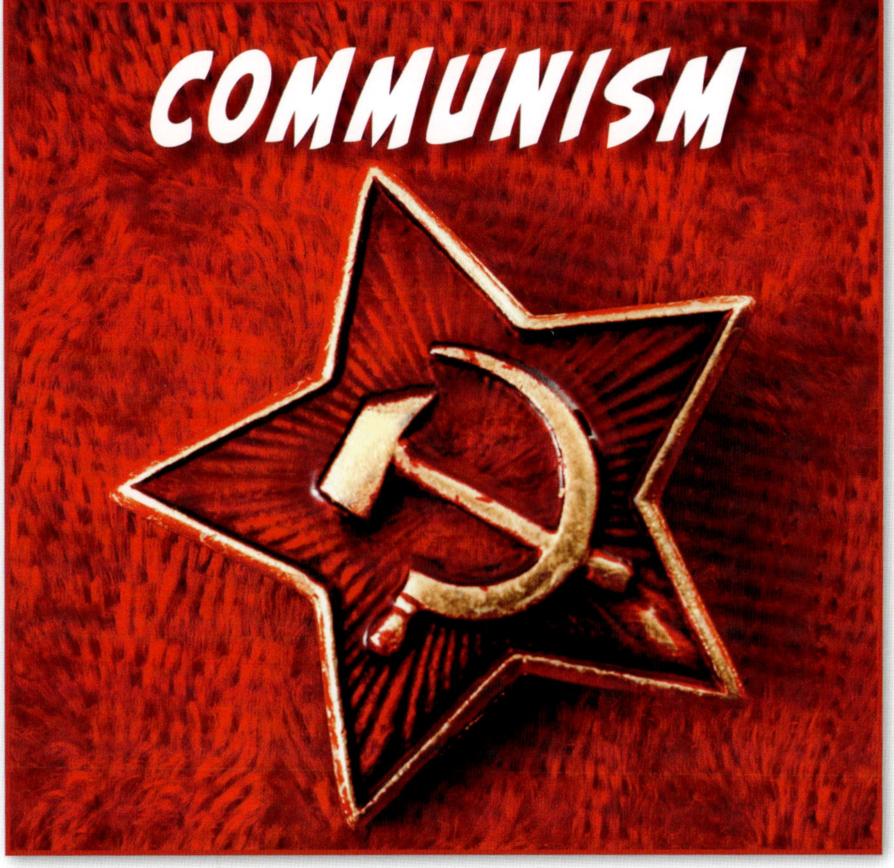

by D. R. Faust

Consultant: Caitlin Krieck, Social Studies
Teacher and Instructional Coach,
The Lab School of Washington

SilverTip Books, an imprint of Bearport Publishing by FlutterBee

Credits
Cover and title page, © Victor Moussa/Adobe Stock; 4–5, © skynesher/iStock; 6–7, © halbergman/Getty Images; 8, © Odua Images/Shutterstock; 9, © Wisnu Gareng/Shutterstock; 10–11, © Historical/Getty Images; 13, © Public Domain/Wikimedia Commons; 14–15, © Artmedia/Alamy Stock Photo; 17, © Public Domain/Wikimedia Commons; 19, © Jacob Wackerhausen/iStock; 20–21, © Photo Josse/Leemage/Getty Images; 23, © Everett Collection/Shutterstock; 25, © emkaplin/Shutterstock; 28, © Oepojo Oepo/Adobe Stock, © Zairi no Design/Adobe Stock, © leremy/Adobe Stock, © Valerie Thang/Adobe Stock, © bonilla1879/Adobe Stock, © MstHazara/Adobe Stock and © Md/Adobe Stock.

Bearport Publishing Company Product Development Team
Kayla Eggert, Theresa Emminizer, Kim Jones, Allison Juda, Cole Nelson, Naomi Reich, Steve Scheluchin, Tiana Tran

Statement on Usage of Generative Artificial Intelligence
Bearport Publishing remains committed to publishing high-quality nonfiction books. Therefore, we restrict the use of generative AI to ensure accuracy of all text and visual components pertaining to a book's subject. See BearportPublishing.com for details.

A Note on Colorization
Some of the historic photos in this book have been colorized to help readers have a more meaningful and rich experience. The color results are not intended to depict actual historical detail.

Library of Congress Cataloging-in-Publication Data is available at www.loc.gov or upon request from the publisher.

ISBN: 979-8-89577-634-6 (hardcover)
ISBN: 979-8-89577-788-6 (paperback)
ISBN: 979-8-89577-722-0 (ebook)

For more information, write to Bearport Publishing, 3500 American Blvd W, Suite 150, Bloomington, MN 55431. Printed in the United States of America.

Contents

Sharing Is Caring

You may have to share things at school. The art room might have only a few colors of paint. They are there for everyone to use. These **resources** are **communal**. When countries share resources with everybody equally, it is called communism.

The word *communism* comes from the Latin word meaning common. The word *community* comes from the same word.

Goods and Means

Communism is a type of **economic system**. This means it is an outline for how a society splits up what it has. This includes the **goods** people use. But it also has to do with the **means of production**. These are the things needed to make goods, such as land and tools.

The means of production are all of the physical things that go into making something. The one thing not included is labor. So, workers are not part of this grouping.

Buildings, such as factories, can be part of the means of production.

Most countries today have **capitalist** economies. The means of production are not shared in capitalism. Small groups of people own them. These owners pay workers to make goods. Then, the owners sell the goods to make a **profit**.

A capitalist economy leads to competition. Buyers often have multiple options to pick from.

Capitalism Booms

Many countries became capitalist in the 1800s. This led to a big shift. Factories boomed. Many more goods were being made. The factory owners often became very rich. However, many workers were poor. They did the work but did not share the profit. Many workers wanted things to change.

Before capitalism took off, most people lived on farms. They grew and made what they needed. But factory workers could not keep farms. Suddenly, they needed to buy all of their goods.

Some of the first factories made fabrics.

The Father of Communism

Some poor workers wanted the government to control the land and factories. They thought this would make things more equal. This idea is called **socialism**. Others wanted to make even bigger changes. The German thinker Karl Marx created the modern idea of communism.

In 1848, Marx and Friedrich Engels wrote *The Communist* ***Manifesto***. This book explained their ideas about socialism and communism.

Karl Marx

Marx thought capitalism broke the world into two classes. One group was made of the rich owners. The other class had the poor workers. In his idea of true communism, there would be no classes. Nobody would own anything. And everybody would be equal.

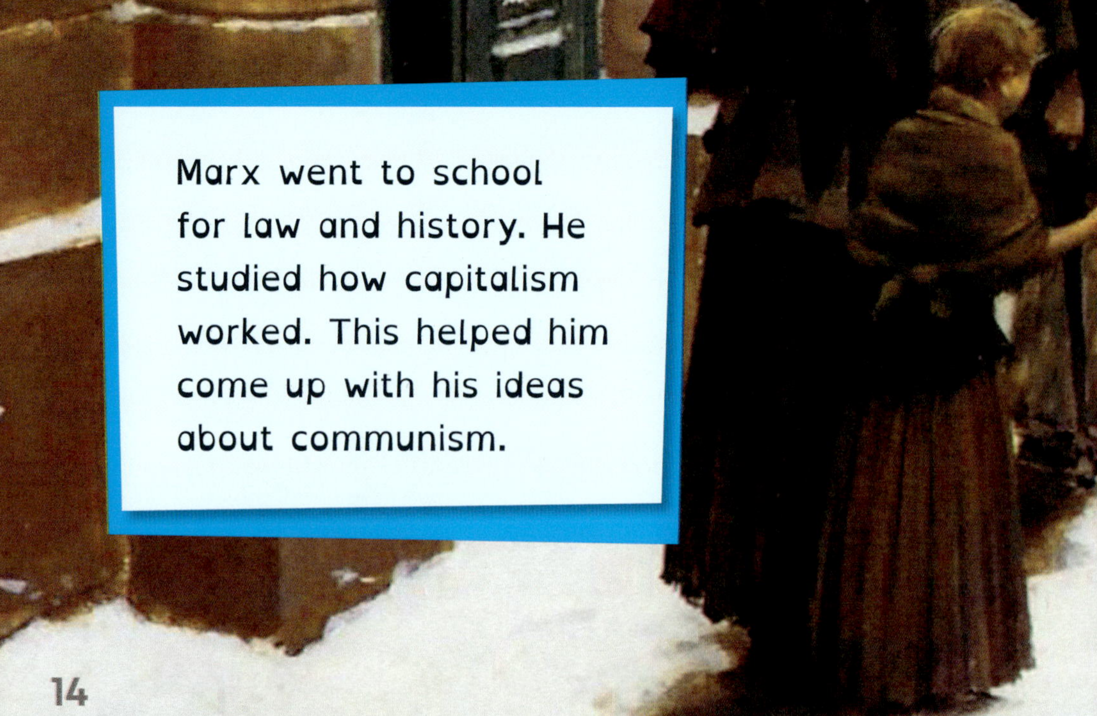

Marx went to school for law and history. He studied how capitalism worked. This helped him come up with his ideas about communism.

Getting to Communism

According to Marx, communism was possible. To get from capitalism to this new system would take two steps. First, the workers would have to take over the government. Then, the people would get rid of the government. From there, everything would be shared.

Marx's ideas were not popular everywhere. He had to move out of Germany after writing his manifesto. He lived in Great Britain for the rest of his life.

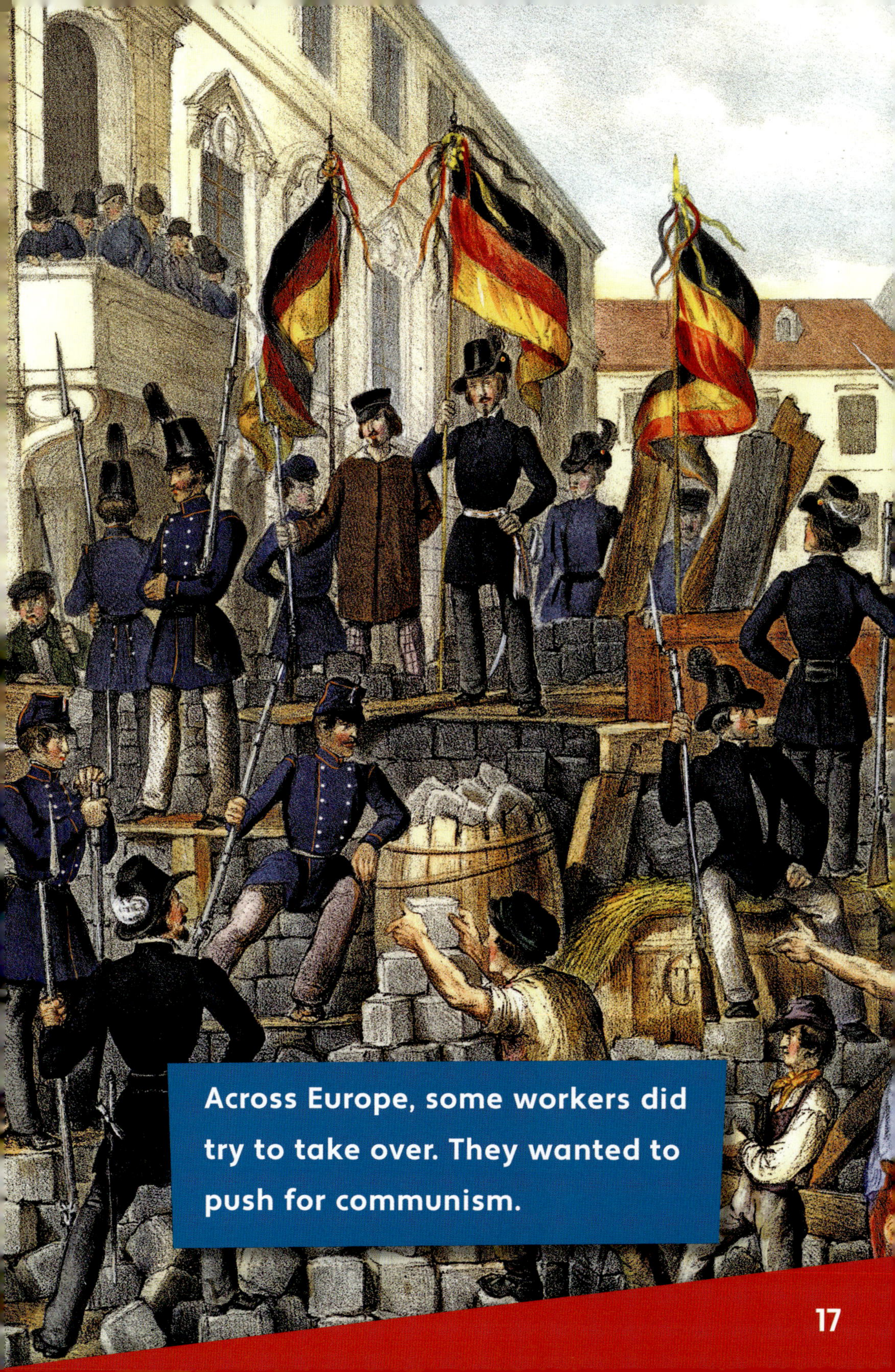

Across Europe, some workers did try to take over. They wanted to push for communism.

In true communism, Marx thought people should not have to work for money. Instead, everybody would do what they really wanted. They would get the goods and services they needed whenever they needed them. He thought this would let people focus on art and science. They could do this instead of making things for people to sell.

The United States had many communist and socialist towns in the 1800s. But most lasted for only a few decades.

Soviet Communism

In 1917, a group of Russian communists were unhappy with how the leader was running things. They rose up and took over the government. Russia then joined with other nearby countries. They formed the Soviet Union. This new country set up a communist system.

Vladamir Lenin formed the Russian Communist Party in 1912. In his system, everyone worked for the government.

The Soviet Union's communism was not like Marx suggested. There was still a government. It was run by powerful leaders. And this government owned all the factories and farms. The people had nothing. And they had little say in their government.

Marx's ideas for communism made sure everyone got what they need. But this did not happen in the Soviet Union. Millions of people there had very little food for many years.

Vladimir Lenin was the Soviet Union's first leader.

Communism Spreads

The Soviet Union tried to spread communism. It helped other governments around the world turn communist. But the system did not last long in most countries. The Soviet Union itself broke up in 1991. Most Soviet countries then became capitalist.

Each communist country works a little differently. But most use a form of communism similar to the Soviet Union's system.

Cuba became communist under leader Fidel Castro.

Communism Today

Today, there are only five communist countries. However, other countries use a system called democratic socialism, which pulls from Marx's ideas. They try to spread wealth more equally. But small groups often own the means of production. In many ways, the ideas of communism still shape parts of our world.

Most of today's communist countries are in Asia. China is the biggest of these. The smallest is Laos.

Modern Communist Countries

Communism vs. Capitalism

The idea of communism was a response to capitalism. How are the economic systems different?

	Capitalism	Communism
Who owns the land and factories?	A person or private company	The people
How are resources split?	People work to buy resources	Everybody shares all resources
Are there rich and poor classes?	Yes	No
What is one example today?	The United States	Cuba

SilverTips for SUCCESS

 SilverTips for REVIEW

Review what you've learned. Use the text to help you.

Define key terms

capitalism
communism
economic systems
means of production
socialism

Check for understanding

Explain what is included in the means of production.

What are the main differences between capitalism and communism?

How has communism been used in practice?

Think deeper

How might your life be different if the economic system in use changed in your city, state, or nation?

★ SilverTips for TAKING TESTS

- **Make a study plan.** Ask your teacher what the test is going to cover. Then, set aside time to study a little bit every day.
- **Read all the questions carefully.** Be sure you know what is being asked.
- **Skip any questions** you don't know how to answer right away. Mark them and come back later if you have time.

Glossary

capitalist an economic system where the means of production are owned privately

communal shared by members of a group or community

economic system the way a society divides up goods and services as well as the means of production

goods things that are made to be bought and sold

manifesto a written statement that explains the goals and opinions of a person or group

means of production the things needed to create goods and services

profit money gained from selling a good or service after all expenses have been paid

resources supplies and materials needed to do something

socialism an economic system where the means of production are owned by the government

Read More

Boothroyd, Jennifer. *Making Money (Personal Finance: Need to Know).* Minneapolis: Bearport Publishing, 2023.

Klepeis, Alicia. *China (Countries).* Mendota Heights, MN: Focus Readers, 2025.

Van, R. L. *Russia (Countries).* Minneapolis: Abdo Publishing, 2023.

Learn More Online

1. Go to **FactSurfer.com** or scan the QR code below.
2. Enter "**Communism**" into the search box.
3. Click on the cover of this book to see a list of websites.

Index

About the Author

D. R. Faust is a freelance writer of fiction and nonfiction. They live in Queens, NY.